CW01091063

AESTHETICS
OF
LANDSCAPE
ARCHITECTURE

RICARDO STERN

FLOXTERRA
EDICIONES

TABLE OF CONTENTS

CHAPTER I
THE AIM OF ART

Materializar lo espiritual hasta hacerlo palpable; espiritualizar lo material hasta hacerlo invisible: ése es todo el secreto del arte.

Jacinto Benavente[1].

Art is a product of the human spirit. This fact makes it radically different from any merely mechanical product, either from man himself as nature or from other areas of nature. What impulses the artist to create his work is an irrepressible desire to make obvious the ineffable, the infinite. What moves him is a secret

---

[1] *Conferencias,* 1924. To materialize the spiritual until making it tangible; to spiritualize the material until making it invisible: that's all the secret of art.

need to leave something of himself in the material world, to alter somehow and try to improve the physical realm, as to leave at least a footprint of his walk through this creation. And not only a mark, but a durable and beautiful one.

> *Sculpte, lime, cisèle ;*
> *Que ton rêve flottant*
> *Se scelle*
> *Dans le bloc résistant !*

What the artist looks for is to give reality to his dreams and fantasies, to leave in his work his entire soul, his own summary of universe and life, idealized by a secret memory of perfection which, though perhaps never seen in real world, is somehow recorded in his spirit.

But matter is, as the Gautier's poem says, resistant and hard; it refuses to be molded by the spirit; from where it follows that art is also a battle between the artist and his material, between ideality and reality, and it ends, if the artist is victorious, with the fusion of these two

---

² T. Gautier, *Emaux et Camées. (L´Art)*

worlds in a single piece that touches both shores as a bridge. And the sense of sublimity in the spectator is to step on this bridge that, starting in his own familiar material world, touches on the other side the shore of the infinite.

Lessing thinks that the ultimate aim of science is truth, while the ultimate aim of art, "on the contrary", is pleasure. Leaving aside for a moment the prejudice that leads this famous thinker to oppose truth and esthetical pleasure, as if they could not exist together, let's think for a moment in his proposition. ¿What is understood here as "pleasure"? It cannot be, of course, the simple pleasure of comfort and bodily enjoyment, since then art would have no objectivity nor stability, nor value in itself, but only as determined by the subjective appreciation of different people. It cannot be either the pleasure produced by pure expression, not mattering at all the ideological or moral contents, for then, as Hegel says, art would be nothing but "an echo, a harmonious tongue; a living mirror where all feelings and passions come to be reflected". But art is something more than that, and the pleasure it provides is also something more. It is, I believe, the pleasure to know for an instant that there is something better than this reality, than this highly technical world, wildly heartless, sadly mechanized, noisy, imperfect, without order or personality. The pleasure bestowed by art is to enter for a moment, through the gate of our familiar matter, but mystically disrupted, to the world of spirit, which is the realm of the personal and individual, of glory and divinity. It's the refined pleasure of airing in a momentary catharsis, at least, the ugliness I find in almost everything, even in my deep self.

Now, if reality, imperfection and untidiness are the things to be escaped from, it's a sound deduction that art has to imbue in us a feeling of ideality, perfection and order, all of which conform what we call beauty. So it's a sound deduction also that beauty must be the very soul of art.

Because beauty is an ideal, it cannot relate with the merely commercial, monotonous and everyday issues. It has to be far away from the vulgar and the merely useful. This is precisely what beauty helps us run away from. "Art is somehow a critique of reality". This is what Graf thinks, and it's quite true. By showing intuitively the opposite of the ephemeral and vane, it remarks to what extent the world could be better.

Taking this definition, and playing a little with words and concepts (just playing, don't be scared), we could say that in a sense, Architecture is the highest of arts. Because, if the goal of art is to create a better world, which of the arts is more suitable for that than architecture? Because the others create *the illusion* of a better world, while this last helps to produce *in fact* a better world. The better world of a string quartet or a piano piece exists only from the ears inside. The better world of a novel exists only in the mind, but the better world of a park or a building exists in objective reality.

But this is only a play of words, for by the same definition of the goals of art, architecture can also be put in the last place of the list. And this is precisely due to it's participation in the real world: it will never reach the highest peaks of ideality. It really transforms the world, and certainly improves it, but it will always be subject to the physical laws and needs of reality, which limit significantly it's possibilities.

In architectural works, the beautiful must join the useful and safe, which can tend to make it a little less beautiful. These works are "fatally predestined" to serve many other purposes that have nothing or little to do with the aesthetical. And these contacts with the mercantile and everyday issues certainly can blur part of the beauty. Many architects would not agree with this, but I believe that to assume it as a natural aspect of their art is not only more honest, but also a key to succeed in understanding and getting the best from it.

The art of Landscape Architecture reveals here, surprisingly, as a little less utilitarian art, because although it is as well related with utility and durability, and it is also limited by the physical and biological laws, it often serves a more purely aesthetical intention than general architecture, since gardens, parks, fountains, etc., can be mainly considered *ornaments* of buildings and cities, and not properly *useful* places or objects. And besides, if the goal of art is to get us closer to paradise, ¿which art will be better that that of *creating paradises*?

But not every garden is a work of art, of course, because they were not always designed with the aesthetical as a priority. This is in fact the difference between horticulture (close to agriculture) and landscape architecture. Both professions deal with the design of green areas and outer spaces, but the primary intention of each one of them is slightly different. For the horticulturist the most important element of a garden are the plants themselves. He or she is moved by a passion for vegetal beings. He is interested, before everything, in designing a *place for plants*, in which they can live healthily and well exposed. His interest is more botanical than artistic, we could say. I'm not saying this is wrong; in fact, it is a valid and interesting approach to making a garden, and there are certainly many plants very worthy in themselves. But pure horticulture will seldom produce a complete work of art.

For the landscape architect, plants and other materials are only elements of design, but the main focus is on a harmonious, coherent project in which everything will take it's own place according to the contribution it makes to the whole. The elements of the work have little value alone, but only in virtue of it's participation in the total effect.

This total effect corresponds to the initial landscaping intention, which could have come from the architect's wish of recreating an idealized childhood garden, for example, or evoke a mysterious and distant country feeling, or a desire to recall nature or whatever. The great inspirations belong to the genius, and he alone knows (maybe not even he) where they come from.

Now, just to make clear a point, I mentioned the recall of nature as one of the inspiration sources, but being careful not to mistake recall with copy. To copy nature is both impossible and useless in art. In fact, by definition, we could say at least in one sense that art is the opposite of nature. But art must be done naturally, which is different. Good works of art seem to have been made effortlessly, though that is almost never true. It must look as if it just couldn't have been any other way, as if molded by inexorable forces, as happens in nature. But to try to copy nature in a garden for example, will only produce a failure, and failure can never be beautiful. So it must be discarded as one of the ends of art to imitate nature perfectly, but rather it must be considered it's supreme end to mold nature in order to make it express ideas, that is, to give it personality, spirituality and intention which, in fact, is to exceed nature itself. Hegel expresses this unsurpassably:

"God obtains much more honor and glory from the activities of spirit than from the products of nature; because not only there is something divine in man, but indeed the divine manifests in him under a much higher form than in nature. God is spirit and, consequently, man is his true intermediary and his organ. In

16

nature, the means by which God is revealed is of purely exterior existence. What is not conscious of itself is inferior in dignity than the self conscious."[3]

So, summing up, let's repeat that the beginning of every work of art, and thus of landscape architecture, is a clear aesthetical intention. In the case of this last art, the intention must sprout from three sources: a) the site, b) the needs and ideas of the client, and c) the artistic inspiration of the architect.

The first cannot be changed; it's certainly a limitation, but also a challenge and a suggesting path for the artist to follow. There will be sites that contribute with their natural beauty to the design, while others will have no interest on themselves and will require a great amount of improvement.

The second, that is, the client's needs and ideas can, and should be subject to revision by the architect. It could well be that the client thinks he needs something he really doesn't, or

---

[3] Hegel. *Of beauty and it's forms (Aesthetics)*

has ideas and concepts that can be enhanced by the professional advice. But finally, the owner of the place will have the last word. A wise owner will listen to advise, but many of them won´t. Besides, sometimes it could happen that he or she has good ideas and (why not?) maybe even better than the architect´s, so if this last wants to be wise also, he will try to be sensitive and humble to receive such ideas and consider how to incorporate them among his own ones.

As regarding the third, the inspiration, there are no clear rules to acquire it. It´s an innate talent every artist should carry with him and that, naturally, is subject of improvement with training and experience. We´ll abound on this on the chapter dealing with the spiritual principles of art.

Once clearly established the intention, it´s required to know deeply the technical and aesthetical principles that will lead to the realization of it. This we´ll talk about on following chapters

.

CHAPTER II

PHYSICAL PRINCIPLES OF ART

Every art, to be art, requires a solid technical knowledge of it's own materials to get to the perfection that beauty demands, since there's no beauty without perfection. You could have great ideas about how a piano piece should be played, but if you don't transmit that to your fingers, if they just can't move the way you want, then all your ideas can go to the trash can. In contemporary aesthetics it's often found a kind of scorn towards the technical aspect of art. You can just drop paint haphazardly in a canvas, and still you're making art. This comes from the mistake of taking creativity and originality (in the best cases) with art. Art is difficult, and there's a hard technique which should be mastered before achieving any deep aesthetical result.

One could reply: art is not only a matter of physical technique. And he'll be right. It's not *only* a matter of technique, but it all hangs and depends on good technique in the first place. When material technical perfection is achieved, the artist's work is only beginning, that's quite true, and so it is that it'll never properly begin without it. It still remains ahead a long way, that is, the aesthetical and spiritual part, which is the visible surface of the work of art. But the physical technical part is the support of that surface, is what makes it stand in it's place. In summary, this technique is what allows the artist to make the reality reflect his fantasy.

Reality is, as we have seen, hard to mould, it presents resistance to conform to the will of the artist; but with proper physical technique, which comes from hard study and long experience, he will succeed in his task. He will conquer the physical world and raise it to the spiritual.

In the case of Landscape Architecture, we have to be aware that there is also a very demanding technical challenge if we want our gardens and landscapes to be useful, lasting, safe and comfortable, assuming that only then we can think of beauty. These aspects are not beauty, but they make it possible.

Since the scope of these essay is mostly aesthetical, and it's not intended to be a technical handbook, we will not go deeply into these physical aspects of technique, but only to mention briefly some of it's most important issues.

For usefulness, for example, we have to pay attention on how roads and paths are laid, vertically and horizontally, how steps are measured, how the space is graded and arranged, how good and practical is the accessibility to different areas, how will the water features work, where will be places to sit, lunch, etc., how the illumination will be designed, and many other things.

For comfort we have to know very well, before everything, which are the human parameters and standards for wellbeing and relaxation; then you have to design taking into account and managing the sun radiation and deep shades, microclimates, wind direction, intensity and temperature, reflections, smells, materials and colors that produce heat or cold and different psychological effects, relative humidity, dry and rainy seasons, etc.

For safety and durability, the skilful architect has to consider the correct calculations for structures such as retaining walls, decks, terraces, etc. He has to take into account also the soil erosion, the efficient drainage design, the appropriate selection of materials and mixtures, irrigation systems, and the health of plants, which is achieved by first selecting adequate vegetation for the local weather, by providing good soil and exposure, good fertilization and pest control, good combination of specimens, etc. In one word, good horticulture. This will, naturally, affect as well the overall beauty of the place.

The good Landscape Architect should also consider, especially in huge projects, ecological issues when designing, such as removing or preserving existing trees, drainage disposals, organic horticulture, how will his project affect the local environment, flora and fauna, how to manage wastes, etc.

And, among all these, he must not forget economy. He has to consider every way to make the project less costly; that is, to make the best for the less, if he's to be ethical with his clients. This is one of the main purposes of engineering calculations, just to take an example. If everything is well calculated it will be safe but fair and without squander.

A last technical thing that the Landscape Architect must not forget is to follow and comply with all the local urban development style, plans and rules. Other arts don't usually cope with this kind of limitations nowadays, but architecture and landscaping do have to submit to these laws, which can even be seen as another challenge instead of a restriction.

Once all this is mastered, the aesthetical job can begin. Up to this point, who dominates these aspects could be a very good engineer or horticulturist, but not yet an *artist* of the outside spaces. He or she will have now to master the second and third part of the abilities needed to become a true landscape architect.

CHAPTER III

AESTHETICAL PRINCIPLES OF ART

A German critic used to say that to understand beauty means to possess beauty[4]. So it's important that if someone wants to produce beauty, he should first try to understand the principles of it. I consider that the principles of beauty can be divided into two parts: first, some technical, learnable and even mechanical principles that, properly used cannot fail to produce, in a certain way, the beauty we're looking for. And second, the giving to the work spiritual aspect, a character. The first principles mentioned must not be confounded with the physical principles just seen in last chapter. These new principles are also technical rules,

---

[4] Lubke

but directly related with aesthetics, and not with utilitarian issues.

But the result these principles can afford, it can't be yet properly called beauty, for it's still not complete. It's somewhat insufficient, as lacking something, just as when you see a "good" thing than cannot be criticized, but it's still not completely convincing. You cannot always say exactly what it is, but the feeling of incompleteness is still there. The object complies with all the rules, but nevertheless it's still not breathtaking. This mysterious think so difficult to explain or name, is the second aspect of beauty: the spiritual principles, which, since they can't be reduced to mechanical rules even by definition, are very difficult to describe. These we'll discuss about in the next chapter.

As regarding the aesthetical principles, they will be studied now to try to understand what rules must be followed to accomplish a good design. First, we have to divide these aesthetical principles into 2 kinds: the first deal with the general *character* of the work, while the others have to do with the *form* of it, that is, the way *elements* are arranged.

The *character* principles are:
- Perfection
- Unity
- Elegance

And the *formal* principles are:
- Harmony
- Balance
- Tension

Let's see each one of them in detail:

1.- Perfection

Bonum ex integra causa; malum ex quocum-que defectu[5], says the old scholastic axiom. A really good thing, whatever it is, must be good in every part, *id est*, perfect, because it would suffice a little defect to make the thing become bad. Some may say that this is an old fashioned and too purist definition, but it applies, I believe, to every age. It can vary what we understand by good or bad, but it is always true that a bad thing among the good makes the good become bad. This means that the artist has to pay attention to every detail, aiming to perfection in everything. In fact, a little defect in an otherwise beautiful work, is more notorious than a huge defect in a faulty work. It´s much worse a single fly floating in a delicious soup, than tenths of them flying around the garbage can. There´s a strange law which establishes that a little imperfection among perfection, will always call the attention much more than the surrounding perfection. The ethimological meaning of the word "perfection" is "to do

---

[5] The good is so in every part; the bad is so for one single defect.

something thoroughly". This denotes that you have to work meticulously, exhaustively, taking care of details. So "perfection" is antonym of "mediocrity"; it's also flawlessness. And the definition of flaw or defect is: "lack of something necessary for completeness".

So this means that when you make a work, you have two options: to make a mediocre, second-rate product, on which all your faulty technique can be diluted and dissimulated; or to attempt to make a masterpiece of perfection, for which you need a great dedication and ability.

I know it sounds pretentious, but that's your goal, if you seriously want to be an artist. Art has to evoke, as we already showed, a better world; it has to be a rapture to a place where mediocrity and stupidity are not the prevailing values, and where nothing seems out of control or disastrous.

In landscaping, as in the other arts, this applies pretty well. We work with nature, but *in order* to escape from some of the natural imperfections, such as diseases, hazardous growing, discomfort, unwelcoming weather, etc. In summary, the utopian goal of gardening is to create paradises on earth, and that demands a serious commitment with perfection.

There's only one way to get to perfection, or at least close to it: criticism. To critizice a work is to try to make it break down, to look carefully, almost obsessively, to the minor failure it could have. You have to be self critic first, and also receive even the hardest attacks from external judges. If you can bear this, you're in the right path to improve your skills. Like someone said: "The most difficult part of art is to learn to see", and it's true. At first, the beginner or amateur sees everything good. Especially in gardening, where the materials themselves are usually beautiful, every garden seems to be "good" or "pretty". But through the development of your sense of criticism, which comes mainly from other critics that judge your work, you gradually start to perceive many faulty or not-so-beautiful details. The aim is to get after some time to be very strict in your judgments, even to the point that you will come to think, as Victor Hugo, that the true masterpiece is a kind of miracle.

Critics are often seen as weird, bitter people, but a good critic will be severe (though fair), and his intention will be to produce at last a good harvest from the artist. There are, of course, bad critics who are usually frustrated artists that, envious of the talent of the true ones, only want to destroy their confidence and make them end up as bad art critics as them.

But, however, think always of the criticism as an opportunity to test your work. You have nothing to lose, for if the work remains and stands over, it will be even stronger after the critique, and if it falls down, it wasn't good enough anyway.

2.- Unity

Unity can be defined as the factor that makes the diversity become a single thing. It can be identified with the essence of the object or, in this case, work of art; that is, some quality that permeates all the components of it and gives them a sense as parts of a whole. Without this quality, the work would't be a single work but a collection of pieces, each one independent to the others.

The essential factors of unity are: the homogeneous material (as, for example, language in literature, tonality in music, materials, forms and colors in visual arts, etc.); main perspective (as, for example, the point of view of the narrator in a novel, or the central perspective in a picture); and the closed character of the work of art (the work creates a world apart and existing on it's own, with it's own place, time, rhythm, rules, etc.). These three factors can be reduced to the following concepts, respectively: *homogeneity, coherence and totality.*

In the last instance, unity depends on the personality of the artist and the idea behind the work. They both will model the whole work into a homogeneous, coherent and total piece. But there are, however, some aesthetical "rules" to attain a certain amount of unity, which, without personality and idea, will be incomplete anyway. Let us review these three main concepts of unity in relation with gardens and landscape architecture work.

Homogeneity: As we saw, this quality is achieved by using the same materials, colors, textures and features in the house, the garden and the environment, whenever possible. That is, to try to combine well the elements according to their origin, function, form, or any other pattern.

Coherence: Coherence means, in few words, a strong sense of consistency and rationality to reach given purposes. This is related to perspective in the sense that everything should be arranged to produce a congruent "picture" in which every element has it's own aesthetical function to produce a determinate effect. It is to submit everything to huge ends. In landscaping, this can be achieved by incorporating the different areas and elements by means of paths, stairs, bridges, light and shade patterns, plants, water features, etc., to get a unified space in which everything contributes to the main objective, such as driving the eye towards beautiful vistas, or to center all the project in a main, fundamental feature (as a pond or fountain, old tree, flower bed, sculpture, etc.), or to make smooth transitions between the different areas of the garden. In summary, if coherence is to be realized, you can't leave any single element or area apart from the whole plot, as if by accident it came to be there. Everything has to be justified in relation to the main objectives. In good art nothing seems to be capricious or haphazardous. Even if these last appear, it has to be done purposedly and well planned.

Totality: As we mentioned, every garden is like a world apart, on it's own. It differs from the surrounding nature and gardens in that it's shaped by a particular idea that cannot be repeated, at least not exactly, anywhere else. It has it's own theme, it's own patterns and rhythm. The rhythm is a very important concept. In the original greek it means a flow, a cadence. It implies regularity and is very much related to symmetry. But here it interests us because it's related with unity. Rhythm gives a strong sense of unity. When you repeat elements with certain regularity, when the whole landscape has a "cadence" of shapes, colors, paths, etc., the place is unified. When a theme or a concept determines the relative function of every part, the whole is harmonically unified. The borders of the garden also contribute to the sense of totality, by excluding everything that does not belong to the design, and emphasizing what is part of it, just as the frame does with a picture.

It's good to note that all these qualities will be much easier to attain in formal than in informal gardens, but in the first, a little failure will be much more noticeable.

3.- Elegance

Almost everyone will agree that an essential part of beauty is elegance, but what is it? It seems to be the most subjective of all the principles, since elegance is like a slippery concept, which seems to vary according to the epoch and particular taste of the spectator. Some, in an attempt to give to the concept a more stable position, associate it with neatness, clarity, simplicity of expression, as opposite to affectation or pretentiousness. Others see a relationship, on the contrary, with extravagance, luxury and grandeur. Others yet find a link between elegance and fashion, even identifying them.

Maybe the three are somehow right. In a sense, the simplicity tends always to be refined and elegant, no matter the changes in fashion; on the other side, grandeur and majesty, when properly accomplished, in the correct place and not seeming pretentious, always carry with them a kind of elegant sublimity. These two could be called the perennial elements of elegance, while the third, related with fashion, is changeable and even unpredictable.

In few words, and to make all this easier, elegance can be simply defined as refinement. And refinement is the opposite of vulgarity, affectation and rudeness. As simple as that. And the essence of all vulgarity lies in lack of sensation, as the English critic John Ruskin stated.

Nothing can so much harm the true beauty as a tawdry detail, not to say a completely vulgar piece. The beauty has to be, as we already saw, out of the common, as far away as possible from the ordinary and the grotesque, that is, it has to be refined (not pedantic, which can sometimes be mistaken).

Just think of the words refinement and culture. The first evokes a process of cleaning and scraping the impurities and toughnesses, while culture is originally related with the cultivation of the land, that is, a hard process of plowing, amending the soil, seeding, etc. So, following the simile, a refined person has to go through a very hard and slow progression. No one, in his or her natural and wild state, can be an elegant person, and a coarse and wild person, just cannot be a good artist.

We just established that elegance has to do with grandeur, but not with pretentiousness. The first aspect is related with simplicity, and the second with sublimity, both of which concepts will be treated later. But there's also the third aspect of elegance, which has to do somehow with fashion. Let's discuss it here, being aware that this is not an easy task since, on one side, most of us will agree that fashion is an ephemeral and even vulgar thing, that has nothing to do with fine art and beauty. Like Oscar Wilde sharply said: "fashion is usually a form of ugliness so intolerable that we have to alter it every six months." And it's true. In latin languages, the word for fashion (*moda, mode*) comes from *hodie*, that means "today". So fashion is what is right and good today but will be odd and bad tomorrow. And that is never a quality of true beauty. But, on the other hand, it's also true that a new work of art that seems old fashioned, will lose much of it's beauty and interest, as if it were a mere copy of past things.

So fashion cannot be completely rejected. This is why I said it's not an easy task.

How to resolve this contradiction? First, let us understand where fashion comes from and why people tend to follow it. One of the chief reasons for fashion is economy. It is often the mere product of a market that is always looking for and promoting novelties in order to have better sales. And this is not only, of course, in the clothing industry, but in many branches of the economy, especially in those related somehow with "aesthetical products". This is the main impulse of fashion, but there are others, as boredom of the people, creativity of the designers, etc.

When a particular trend seems to draw to its end, because all it's resources are already exploited and worn out, a creative individual or group thinks of something new and starts producing it. This is good in itself, for it brings a fresh approach towards old problems, renovating the interest and throwing out the boredom of the old and known things. As these new proposal starts to spread, a given society adopts it as it's hallmark, which helps to define it and give it personality in opposition to other societies that differ in economical position, time, place, etc. So a very important function of fashion is to *separate* one group from another. But if you belong or want to belong to this new group, you have to adopt it's fashion obligatorily, for if not, you will be excluded, or, as Lord Chesterfield stated: "If you are not in fashion, you are nobody"[6]. In this sense, fashion carries out the function of *linking* the individual with the group he wants to be accepted in. So there's at the same time a separation and a linking function of these trends.

But at the end, the cycle will close: a new generation or group will come with a new vogue, and if you want to be accepted by them, you will have to abandon your old fashion and adopt their new one. If not, you'll start to be considered an "elder", or a weird person, and since there's people that does not want to be treated as such, they'll be forced as slaves to

---

[6] *Letters*, April 30, 1750

follow the new fashion. Unless you are a true genius, with a personality strong and interesting enough as to impose a new fashion. But this is not common, so you'll most probably have to yield in some manner. But, even yielding, you have three choices, if we agree with A. Dufresne:

> La nullité suit la mode,
> la prétention l´exagère,
> le gout pactise avec elle.[7]

You can choose to simply follow and surrender completely to the force of fashion. Or you can take the fashion and exaggerate it with coarse pretentiousness, or you can tastefully negotiate with it. But what means to "negotiate" with fashion? I think it means to take some of it´s advices, especially those most likely to be solid and permanent, and those that bear quality and dignity within themselves, while leaving aside the lowest products of that particular

---

[7] *Pensées, maximes et caracteres,* 11. Stupidity follows fashion, / pretentiousness exaggerates it, / good taste negotiates with it.

vogue, and replacing them with the products of your own personality and the perennial values of elegance and good taste. In this way, like in any pledge, you are accepting something, but also imposing something on the other part. This way you will be neither a slave of fashion, nor an enemy of it, but a partner, working together with it for the benefit of both parts.

This will lead to another concept, half the way between the extremes of pure and vain fashion, on one side, and rigid, static, even pedantic classicism in which beauty is seen as perennial even in it´s external form, and where it tends to be somewhat tedious and lackluster, not to say apocryphal. This halfway concept, more stable than fashion but less static than classicism is called artistic style of a given time, which shouldn´t be confused with the personal style of the artist, which will be studied in the next chapter.

The artistic style of a given time is a kind of aesthetical trend of more refined and long-lasting values than common fashion. It is modernity, often healthy to beauty, mixed with personality of the individual artists, who "breath" and "swim" in the modern environment of art, but never using other's lungs or arms to do it.

This is respecting the third part of elegance, but let's now treat the other two everlasting values of it. The first is Sublimity, which has to do with greatness and majesty. It's something that goes above limits in a sense. It's the feeling of the infinite through the material, as we saw in chapter I, and it generates astonishment, enthusiasm and reverence.

The sublime or majestic can be produced by two different "moods": A) An example of the first would be a reposed extension, as the ocean or sky (speaking of nature), or a tranquil, spacious pond, or a quiet and large lawn area (speaking of landscaping). In this sense, it is related with *sobriety* and *austerity*. B) But sublimity can also be produced by the force of a powerful being, as a thunderstorm or blaze, or the passions of a hero, for example. In this other sense it has to do with *drama* and *power*.

The first mood is what Kant calls "mathematical sublimity" (related with extension) and the second is named by him "dynamic sublimity" (related with force).

From this it must be inferred that not every work can be sublime. This is because sublimity is always related with either repose or passion, which form part of the "serious" group of moods. But in art there's also an important place for joy, humor and little scale effects, all of which leave out the sense of sublimity. Every mood has it's own place. There are places and clients rather suited for seriousness, while others not, in landscaping art. Obviously, trying to make a sublime garden in, for example, a 200 square meter area, will only be ridiculous. On the contrary, in that same area, without pretentiousness, you can create a modest but beautiful garden. One must be careful: the ridiculous and kitsch is a very close neighbor of sublimity. In fact, just one little step short or long of sublimity, will make you fall plainly on the realm of ridiculousness. Oscar Wilde thinks that the tacky is the unsuccessful attempt to be sublime. The French word "cursi" is defined as "what pretends to be refined without really being so".

To avoid this, there's always an accurate remedy, which is the second perennial component of elegance: modesty and simplicity. If you acknowledge your limitations or the site's limitation, you'll be prevented against pretending to reach the sublime and ending in the "cursi". Simplicity is not necessarily, in this sense, want of complexity, but of affectation. It should permeate every good design, either sublime and aristocratic, or more homely, as a rule of thumb.

Recently, there has been an attempt to recover the spirit of simplicity in the so-called "minimalism". The principle is correct, but sometimes it becomes a mere posing, a pretended high spirituality. The true minimalism is an attitude originated as a humbleness of spirit in monasteries or eremites, for example, and can reach truly sublime moments when it is pure and outflowing from a true simplicity of soul and life. But when it is just the imitation of a vogue, it becomes vulgar and monotonous.

Excess of ornamentation, on the other hand, is always a false way to achieve beauty. It's what common people often do to feel elegant, but resulting naturally in the opposite, making the design seem unnatural and deceitful. It's a desperate attempt to fix and mask a poor background, and it shows.

These were the three main principles or rules that affect the *character* of the work of art: Perfection, Unity and Elegance. Let's continue now with the three most important principles that will determine the *arrangement* of the elements, and which are known since antiquity:

4.- Harmony

In a general sense, harmony is the main, not to say the only great material principle of beauty, spanning above the whole work. But in a more limited and technical sense, harmony is related only with the *essential quality* of the materials to be combined, and not with the *distribution or size* of them. The principles related with these last two aspects are symmetry and proportion.

The remote origin of the concept of harmony is a religious and cosmic vision. For the ancient cultures, especially the Greek one, the universe was composed of many different and heterogeneous elements, as the physical, human, and divine. These were not only heterogeneous, but even opposing. And not only opposing one to another, but even each of these elements had opposing principles inside of themselves. Just think about it; the physical world is made of contradictions: fire and water, light and darkness, earth and wind, fury and repose, cold and heat, subtlety and toughness,

etc. The human soul and body are made up as
well of contradictions: love and hate, bone and
flesh, fear and bravery, etc. And even the gods,
in greek mythology, were uneven and hostile
among themselves. But all this heterogeneity
and opposition could, and should exist in a
kind of peaceful and easy consonance for the
universe to work properly. This consonance or
conformity is harmony.

So we can define harmony simply as the
conformity of the heterogeneous into a more
homogeneous unity. So, by this definition,
we'll refuse to understand harmony as a union
of the same. This will never be harmonious,
properly speaking, but only equal. The art of
harmony is to make a *unity out of diversity*. But
we must never confuse oneness with unity.
Unity is necessarily a compound thing, a *union*
of assorted elements, while oneness is a single
thing, or the *repetition* of that single thing,
which in itself can be good and pleasing, but
just as a part of the whole work, since oneness
cannot be alone a work of art, properly speaking, nor a harmonious compound or design.

So the first think that breaks down the harmony is oneness. The second is discord. Returning to the ancient conception of the universe and mythology, there were times when the cosmic harmony was broken, at least momentarily, by one or more of the elements. For example, when the soul of man was in dissonance with the order of the gods, it was called the *sin of hybris,* and it demanded from the gods or the destiny (which was a kind of impersonal god) a punishment to put the human soul in it's place, and balance the cosmic order again. Or sometimes something in the physical world went out of control, altering the harmony of nature momentarily and causing many damages, as an eruption or an earthquake. So we see through these examples that disharmony comes from disorder and from the "collision" of the elements instead of submission of ones to the others, in an inherent hierarchy. This is most obvious in music, where this collision is even physical, when sound waves literally clash in the dissonance.

So, to achieve harmony, the artist should first start to discover which is the natural hierarchy of the different elements he is working with, and then let them settle down in order and peace, so that contraries blend in a "non-clashing unity". But when elements collide? In music, for example, waves collide when you play together very similar and close notes, but with a little difference. The sound waves are not similar enough to be a oneness, nor too distant to be truly different sounds. So, disharmony can be defined as an unsuccessful oneness, or an unsuccessful unity. That is, to try to combine elements that, due to it's diversity, can't conform a oneness, but due to different reasons, among them perhaps similarity, cannot "get well together", either. To understand these "different reasons", is what we'll try to do next, at least in reference to the art of Landscaping.

Strange as it may sound, Landscape elements are extremely heterogeneous. You can have, in a same place, dead and live elements, different colors and materials, pants that come from very distant places of the world and very different soils and climates, plants that grow naturally in creeks, mountains, beaches, deserts.

To attain harmony the designer has to consider the external environment and choose forms, materials, colors and plants that correspond to that region. This is also an ecological issue. He has to consider the urban style, or the local flora, but also the style of the house or buildings to which the garden is related. He has to group plants according to their cultural needs, such as water supply, light exposition, kind of soil, etc. But also, at least to a certain point, according also to their different origins, putting together the Mediterranean plants, the far east plants, etc. (not in a single garden, of course, for it would seem rather a bothanical park). In a single garden a decision has to be made as regarding which style would dominate.

It must be remembered that a very important aspect of harmony is the concept of naturality. The art has to appear as if it could be in no other way, as if an ever-existing idea suddenly came to take material form. When you listen, for example, a Mozart's piece, it seems as if it flowed out without effort from his spirit; as if the music imposed itself to the composer in this way, and as if it existed since eternity and just found a receptive artist to write it down and bring it to material existence. In the case of Mozart, we can suppose it was truly this way, but in the case of others, as Beethoven or Flaubert, we know that it took lots of work and effort to achieve it, but at the end the effect is the same: it seems natural and "unavoidable". And these produces a sense of repose and peace that is an essential part of harmony. In gardening exactly the same happens. A garden must appear to be inevitable and self-existent.

Sometimes you see a garden and it looks somewhat odd, as if it was forced to take this shape. This happens frequently, for example, when plants are altered, through pruning, and compelled to take unnatural, artificial shapes. This happens also when you plant palms in a woodland, or when lots of species are displayed without any property linking them, as in a nursery.

So, in conclusion, harmony is to produce a *homogeneous* effect out of heterogenous elements, but in regard only of it's *qualitative* properties (color, form, texture, hardness, origin...), and not with the *quantitative* ones (size, number, location...).

5.- Balance

This has always been considered one of the two great laws of beauty, along with harmony. It is a kind of harmony itself in the sense that it makes objects get well together, but the difference is that here the important point is to blend elements not in regard of their *essential qualities,* as harmony does, but of position, magnitude, number and mass, which are *quantities.*

Balance is determined by proportion and symmetry, which in fact are the same thing, but with little different connotations. Formerly the terms symmetry and proportion were identical (one coming etymologically from latin, and the other from greek). But in latter aesthetical theories they were differentiated, not always clearly. Ones tried, for example, to uphold that symmetry is based on purely rational, geometric divisions of space, while proportion is less so. But this is not true, since also proportion could be reduced to mathematical formulas, as we'll discuss later. Others have thought that symmetry is comparable with rhythm, both being repetitions or successions of fixed elements in regular intervals, while proportion refers to the dwelling of the elements simultaneously in space. Proportion is more general, meaning the pleasant relation of *portions* with other *portions* (pro-*portione* in latin) or with the whole. Symmetry ("with measure" from the greek symmetria) is to relate things in exact reflecting positions, which is a kind of proportion. So, every symmetrical layout is proportioned, but not every proportion is symmetrical.

The origin of the pleasure given by correct proportion and balance has also been discussed for long. Ones attribute it to a biological and natural instinct, while others relate it with the relaxation that stability and simplicity give, and others still with the spiritual pleasure of seeing reflected a kind of "social order" in the proportionate designs (Lukáks, for example). But what is not on dispute is that it causes great pleasure and tranquility.

The lack of proportion can result in two opposites: meagerness or exaggeration. Both cause a feeling of anxiety and annoyance. To avoid this, many wise scholars through the centuries have tried to find mathematical formulas for proportion. As far as I know, only two have been recognized by mathematicians as truly certain. They are the so called "Golden Section" and the "Plastic Number", the first being known since the ancient Egypt and the second recently discovered in 1928 by a Benedictine monk and architect. This numbers pretend to establish infallible proportions between elements. Whether this be true or not, the problem with them is that their application can be very subjective, since there is no exact rule about that. However, knowing them can sometimes be useful for the Architect, so we'll give them. The "Golden Section" factor is 1.618 and the "Plastic Number" is 1.324, this meaning that if you take an object and you want to combine it with other, the second should be bigger or smaller in this proportion. It applies for dividing the plan, for sizing vertical elements, etc. But, as we mentioned, the application can be very subjective or varied.

In the case of gardens, disproportion is without question one of the most frequent problems. Sometimes people with small spaces want a true woodland inside their yard, which is obviously out of scale. But, actually, what happens much more often is the contrary: gardens suffer from scantiness.

People often forget that correct scale and proportion is a good relationship between elements, which will help to determine the importance and function of each of them, and that it is also a balance that should exist to counteract the preeminence of any given element. So, the first thing to consider is to balance the major element inside of the garden, which is usually the house (though it could be a pond, a great tree, a main path, etc.). In fact, the whole garden could be seen, in these cases, as the balance of the edification(s). So how could it be explained that very often people treat the garden as a mere afterthought, or a kind of accidental decoration of the house?

The beauty of a garden depends to a very high extent on the importance it receives on the whole project. A garden ought to look "as essential to the life lived in that place as is the living room or dining room or kitchen, and often as ample, in size and in furnishings, as what lies withindoors"[8]

And the second most important factor to take into account about proportion is what surrounds the site. If it is a high and ample wooded area, or high buildings, it would be ridiculous to think only of tiny and delicate species to plant (except if the space to garden is tiny). You should resolve all these imbalances with boldness, opposing to the pressing and dominating outside elements at least a couple of equally strong in character elements.

A most important aspect to consider as well is to establish correct proportions between space and mass. Space can be realized with lawns, paved surfaces, distant extended views, large ponds, etc., while mass comes from dense plantings, high and leafy trees, slopes, etc. So,

---

[8] Joe Eck, *Elements of Garden Dessign*

the relation between these elements should be proportioned.

And about symmetry, we can say that it lies so deep inside man's soul, that he has to fight hard when he wants to break it. The natural impulse is to make every design symmetrical and, actually, I can't think of any garden that absolutely breaks with symmetry. At least two containers flanking the house door, or two similar trees reflecting each other, or whatever symmetrical feature you can think of, but there's never a garden without some of it.

Some think symmetry is "out of fashion", or that it belongs only to very formal outlines, but that isn't completely true. Of course, that it's most natural place is in those kinds of designs. But even the most informal intention has to have a certain degree of symmetry if it doesn't want to produce an annoying and, paradoxically, an unnatural result. Why unnatural, someone could ask, if nature is not symmetrical, but contingent? But this comes from the ordinary mistake that nature is not symmetrical. Look at the flowers, for example, not to say the animals, or the snail shells. So, in nature, random and accidental forms are combined with the most perfect examples of symmetry and geometry, as should also be in good gardens. Of course, this implies that excess of symmetry isn't desirable, either. And this is not any new theory, but even Plotinus, the 3rd century roman philosopher, pointed out that there is a lack of life, and a merely mechanical, instead of organical, unity in the strict application of the concept of symmetry. It simply lacks tension and interest.

So, in conclusion and returning to balance, we must be concerned to achieve it always, whether in a symmetrical or asymmetrical way. In this last case, you must balance the elements taking into account their visual weights. You have to know that light colors, for example, tend to make the figure appear bigger, but lighter, while dark colors do the contrary. The elements put in the right side of the perspective will seem heavier that the same elements put in the left; the rough elements are also heavier than the plain, and so are the components that lie close to the edges of the view, especially the nearest. This and some more qualities make the elements visually heavier or lighter, and this must be considered to balance elements and provide always a compensation on the opposite side, either identical (symmetry) or proportional.

In landscaping, balance is even more difficult than in painting or in graphic design, since we deal with three-dimensional space, where, at least in theory, every possible scene should be balanced. And it's even more diffiult in a sense, perhaps, than architecture, since we have to deal also with a fourth dimension, which has a lot to do especially here: time. The garden is composed of live elements that grow and change, and that has to be considered, too.

4.- Tension

For goodness, growing to a pleurisy,
Dies in his own too-much.

William Shakespeare, *Hamlet,* Act IV

Once you master the rules of perfection, unity, elegance, harmony and balance, you are ready to start breaking them, if you want to get to a higher level, but there is also an order to be followed for breaking well the rules. In other words, there are rules to break the rules. We'll try to find them out, but first it would be good to try to understand the principles lying behind the aesthetical concept of tension.

Tension, generally speaking, is the opposite of relaxation. It implies, thus, concentration. In Spanish, the word for amusement is "diversión", from the latin *Divergere*, which means "to vary, to deviate, to distract". So, when you are concentrated in a job or in anything else, you need periodical distractions to avoid fatigue and exhaustion. You need, in other words, to relax from tension. But on the contrary, pure diversion is flat and can also develop boredom and fatigue, becoming itself a tension. So, in this case you need tension to distract you from distraction; stress to relax from relaxation. This is the third main principle of beauty: to break the evenness and perfection of harmony and balance to give interest to the work. Interest because a perfect layout is very much predictable, and the predictable is less appealing and exciting than what's out of the ordinary and even mysterious. And tension also makes the work seem more human and friendly; perfection, assuming it could really be reached, causes some kind of reverential fear, and appears distant and cold as a quality exclusive of divinity, while some calculated imperfections can help to make the work seem less Olympic, so to say, and closer to the human heart, since humanity is in a sense synonym of imperfection. In one word, a little component of drama is required in almost every true work of art.

So, we could say that in art (a product from men to other men), the hypothetical absolute lack of imperfection would be in itself an imperfection. Or as Francis Bacon states in one of his famous *Essays*[9], "there is no excellent beauty that hath not some strangeness in the proportion". Think of the natural or artificial moles that beautiful women have on one side of the face as a good example of how a tensional and strange element, that could be in itself considered a flaw, can remark and enlarge the beauty.

But this is not all. Tension not only gives the benefits described, but it also helps appear the harmonious and balanced background from which it distinguishes itself as even more unified. And this is because one of the main factors of unity is an opposing external element. What makes a design being a self existent entity is the difference between it and other entities. For example, in a country there could be many internal differences, regarding politics,

---

[9] 43, *Of Beauty*

religion, social issues, etc., but when an external enemy attacks that nation, all the people are usually unified in a common cause, so differences disappear, and to the external viewer, that nation would appear as a great unity. The same happens in art. If you oppose a diverging element to a somehow unified background, this last will appear even more as a unity, or in other words, it's factors of harmony will become clearer. The human eye will look unconsciously for difference and contrast, so if none is clearly provided, it will start to discover little contrasts even in the harmonious combinations, which will start breaking the unity of it. But if you provide an obviously contrasting element, then the eye will settle on it, diluting and attenuating the differences among the surrounding elements and focusing only on the difference between this last as a whole and the single contrasting ingredient.

If the main aim is to drive the attention to a particular point, the first rule is to put it against an even and different backdrop. The second great law is to do it very tactfully. Only one or two contrasting elements will suffice to produce the desired effect, but more will probably do the opposite. Contrast is the exaltation of singleness while harmony and balance are the exaltation of unity, so if you exalt lots of single components, they will stop being so to become a "group of singles", or a new unity, which is now the opposite of singleness. They will not be dissonances anymore, but will become part of the general harmony and balance, so the overall effect will be of disharmony instead of the originally intended contrast. A third rule of contrast is that it should be in such a way to appear intentional. This is the contrary of harmony and balance, in which everything should look natural and effortlessly. But if in Contrast the same effect results, it will look more like an accidental mistake, than an artistic intention or an expressive resource. And a fourth law is to resolve the tensional conflict. In music and drama, where tension is perhaps the most important part, this conflict is almost always resolved by returning to the tonic in the case of non-experimental music, or by leading the conflicting forces into a "happy end", called in greek *homonoia*. But in visual arts, where all the elements exist simultaneously and not in succession, how can you lead to that *homonoia* or peaceful resolution? In the case of gardens and architecture, to say something, simultaneity is not so absolute as in painting or sculpting, since you can go around the work, changing from space to space in succession of time. So, if the garden has, for example, a kind of predetermined route by means of paths, terraces, etc., then you can provide, after a strong contrasting space or element, another peaceful, simple, reposed space for resting the eye.

Now, returning to tension and contrast, there are some academic rules to do it, but none is final and it has to flow from the artist's creativity to completely attain it's effect. The *unpredictable* is what matters.

Conclusion

These are the main and perennial principles or rules that have to be always followed to
produce true, long-lasting beauty. We're not
ignorant, however, that many modern theories
deny this, making of beauty a product of subjective appreciation. In "modern aesthetics"
every fixed referent is dissolved, so beauty becomes a matter of mere personal taste and fashion of the epoch, or experimental creativity
sometimes. But how, then, can art be valued
from an objective and normative point of view,
if every work is subject to the historic relativ-
ity? This is, indeed, a serious dilemma of modern aesthetics, and the only answer they can
give is that actually beauty is not an everlasting
value, leaving without explanation how could
it be possible, then, that people still consider
beautiful the works of Caravaggio or the po-
ems of Virgil, made in a very different fashion
than the current.

In fact, some modern theories tend to consider art a kind of banal thing, in which the

only thing that matters is the external form, the vulgar originality, the vain and arrogant expression without contents. This has been, unfortunately, the center of much contemporary art. *L'art pour l'art*, that sounds so good, is in fact what brought many trends of mainstream art to a deplorable condition of which it seems to be slowly getting out. Art has been sometimes, in the end of 20th century, nearly dying of arrogance, pretentiousness and want of true spirituality.

So, these reviewed principles are not enough, since they don't deal with spiritual values, but cannot either be despised, for they are the second floor of the building of art. The first are the physical principles and the third and last are the spiritual principles. If one of the first two is missing, the third cannot exist either, and if the third is the missing, the other two can exist, but the building will be incomplete.

The last chapter of this brief essay will be a difficult one, since it's also a modern trend to deny even the very existence of that untangible thing that we've been calling spirit, almost always due more to a misconception of what it is than to a true religious or philosophical logic, as is pretended. So, we'll have to start by defining it first, to dissipate some doubts and then proceed, if we succed to clear them sufficiently, to apply our deffinitions to art, and above all, to the art of Landscape Architecture.

CHAPTER IV

SPIRITUAL PRINCIPLES OF ART

Das Schöne ist wesentlich das Geistige, das sich sinnlich äussert, sich im sinnlichen Dasein darstellt.

G. W. F. Hegel[10]

The true beauty of great art is the invisible but not less real part that hides behind the physical and aesthetical aspects of a work. This is the part that cannot be reduced to formulas, nor criticized according to rules, or vogue or "good taste". It's the depth of the whole work, the human part.

---

[10] *Religions Philosophie*, I. The beautiful is essentially the spiritual, that externalizes materially and is present in the material being.

The physical world is mechanical. Everything happens as the effect of a cause; everything obeys unbreakable laws. It's like a clock working inexorably, without will nor personality. The human soul has also a mechanical part (that which is studied and controlled by psychology) that reacts to the stimulus according to determinate laws. But there is also a part of the human beings, deeper inside, that has a free will and that doesn't react predictably nor submits itself to mechanical regulations. This part, called sometimes conscience and sometimes spirit, is what makes humans different from every other creature on the world, and is what gives them a kind of divine proportions, so to say.

The mechanical is cold, impersonal, general, while the spiritual is always personal, unique and particular. The higher the level of spirituality, the higher the personality. Personality is the opposite of the mere technique, of imitation and following the crowd.

Our present world seems sometimes to be just the contrary. It tries to uniform everything, to minimize the personal, to reduce everything to technical, methodized procedures, to impose a common thought and language, etc. So more than ever, art is in the obligation of counterbalancing these trends through providing a deeply personal and humanistic response. More than ever, spiritual maturity is required from the artists.

The spiritual contents of a work of art can be defined simply as what is symbolically presented in the artistic (external) form. In this sense, every not-empty work of art can be seen as a symbol that represents something else (as all symbols), and this "something else" is precisely the spiritual contents, which can be an emotion, an idea, a moral teaching, a personal statement.

But since this is the subjective, non technical and untangible part of art, it can't be appreciated by everybody, as the physical or aesthetical parts, which are easy to perceive and judge, according to some objective, even mathematical rules sometimes. But the spiritual part can only be recognized and apprehended by someone in the same "tuning" or spiritual range of the artist. Or, in other words, someone that has something to add of his own to the work. So, the deep content will tend to be a secret for the majority.

This is the reason why some modern art has often been so distant and even hostile to the public, because in it the content and the form have been separating more and more, producing, on one side, vane and empty forms without spiritual contents that cannot completely satisfy; and on the other side, producing a purely intellectual, ideological art that cannot satisfy either and cannot even be called properly art, no matter how interesting it's contents may be; for as we've repeated many times, art is the union of both aspects. So, the spiritual maturity in art would be to know that pure ideology without following some rules to get good forms is not art, and pure external form without any "message" from the artist's spirit is, in the best cases, a beautiful shell or a merely technical achievement. But this is only the first step of spiritual ripeness. When the artist has understood this, then he she has still in front a very long path to develop a solid spiritual cultivation and development. No matter how good may he or she be to print his personality in the artistic form if his personality is poor and wearisome. And only the years, the suffering, the sensibility, the enrichment of his soul through the highest and most sublime works of art, the forging of a strong moral and intellectual character will give him something interesting to put in his art. There are no shortcuts, excepting maybe, and that I say doubting, for the very greatest geniuses.

Now, based on the definition of spiritual contents, we can deduce the spiritual principles, although they cannot be taken as rules, since this part is precisely the free and personal part. Yet, we can try to observe great works and, through analysis of their contents, try to determine or at least to intuit some of the spiritual principles that are usually present in most of them. In my opinion, this are the following: Creativity, Emotion, Ideology and Personal Style.

1.- Creativity

In the strict sense of the word, creativity is the faculty of humanity in general or a human being in particular to create. And to create is to produce something new and original. There have been many theories from artists, philosophers, theologians, psychologists, etc., to try to understand where creativity and inspiration come from. Some, from a rather theological point of view, attribute it to divine inspiration, or demonic inspiration, seeing the artist as a kind of medium. This is the origin of the word *enthusiasm,* meaning in Greek "with god inside". Others, from a more psychological point of view, see the process of creation as a gradual ascent from a vague feeling to a detailed explanation and verification of the work. Others still, like Goethe, assign the origin of inspiration to the movements of history, seeing the artist as an interpreter of the spirit of his time. The creativity and originality, in this last case, are seen as a product of the historical situation, and not as a personal achievement.

Whatever theory we take, what is clear is that creativity is related with originality. The first is defined as the capacity of the individual to face new and unexpected challenges, getting to the best and new solutions for them. Originality is the novelty of a work of art. This novelty comes usually from the creativity and personal style of the artist.

We'll return latter to deepen our reflections about originality, but now we'll see what is behind the artist's creativity. First, there is a great sensitivity to perceive the transformations of reality, if he is to react accordingly. Then, the faculty of revising with critical objectivity and boldness the old and insufficient methods or techniques, as well as the exceeded and broken doctrines and ideologies of the past (remembering always, of course, that ideas are never old nor new, but only true or false), in order to adequate them to the present necessities. In other words, the artist has to have always his eyes wide open to discover stiffened up solutions for new challenges, and then risk himself in the trial of new possibilities. So, there is always needed a great amount of boldness, which will take you to heaven or to hell, as an old greek stated. But this risk is much better than mediocrity and cowardice. In art what is needed is, as Danton said in a famous discourse to the French Assembly in 1792, *de l´audace, encore de l´audace, et toujours de l´audace!*[11]

However, this must not be mistaken as a crazy and purposeless originality, looked for at every cost, as if it had a value for itself. Originality is only valuable when it truly comes from an outstanding solution to a new or old problem, from a historic need of innovation and from the personality of the artist. When originality is pursued just for itself, it then becomes an empty, mannered and even vulgar quality of the work. But great original masterpieces, as those of Cervantes, Debussy or Kandinsky, on the contrary, become influential, establishing a new order and rules that go beyond their own time.

---

[11] Boldness, still boldness, always boldness!

Landscaping has suffered perhaps more than any other art the scarceness of creativity. It's not completely absent, evidently, but for any reason, it's progress has been always slower that other arts'. In part it could be because its elements and materials are somehow limited[12], what doesn't happen in literature or music or painting. But possibly the main reason is that gardening isn't usually even treated as a fine art, leaving thus aside the originality and creativity as non-important values.

But they are important, indeed. If you briefly analyze the stiffened and sometimes absurd traditions of gardening, you would be surprised to see how many things are made by default when designing gardens, as if they were even part of the concept of garden itself. For example, a non-written definition of garden, but almost universal in most occidental minds is: "A place with lawn and some

---

[12] The site, the weather, the client's needs, tastes and concerns, the availability of plants and construction materials, etc., are all very heavy limitations.

ornamental plants". This is the common understanding of a garden, but why? A garden without lawn wouldn´t be a garden? Actually, grass was started to be used widely as a garden feature just a couple of hundred years ago (excepting for golf courses and large country estates). The Arabic, the Roman, the colonial or the Japanese gardens, just to mention some, didn´t included lawns, and were very beautiful gardens indeed.

This is just an example, but there are many more. Yet, the aim is not to break paradigms just for a hunger of distinction and originality. The true aim is to be sincere and to express the truth that is in the artist´s spirit. "The merit of originality is not novelty; it is sincerity."[13]

---

[13] T. Carlyle, *Heroes and Hero-Worship*.

2.- Emotion

Every work of art, willing or not, is symbolizing something, but what is it? An idea, a concept? Maybe. But what primarily art is to signify is emotion. To express concepts, there's no better way than discursive, logical language. The only way in which art could help to improve it is by giving some illustrations or examples. But the true, natural place of art, more than the world of ideology, we repeat, is the realm of feelings and emotions. Susanne Langer defines a work of art as an expressive form created for our perception through the senses or the imagination, expressing human feeling. And she helps us to understand what is emotion, making us realize that there is a portion of experience that, although belonging entirely to the human life, it still refuses to discursive formulation (verbal expression). It's what we usually call the subjective aspect of experience, the direct feeling of it: like waking up, moving, being thirsty, etc. Many of these experiences, though very common, are still lacking a name; and even those that have one, are not yet subject to definition or description. Think for example of the emotion called "fear". Can you really describe what is it? No! Every one knows intuitively what is it to be fearful, but there is no way to describe exactly what it *feels*. So, in this point is where art comes to help us, by reproducing inside of us, instead of giving a verbal description, a feeling that was before in the artist's soul.

Why is this so important? The reason is simple: articulate language is very limited to name feelings. There is a surprisingly wide range of emotions that cannot be described, nor have a name. In fact, in a sense, nothing outside of the purely intellectual and discursive could be described, but only evoked. When we say red, we need to know beforehand what is red if we are to understand it. Imagine a blind person reading thousands of times the dictionary definition of red. Will he come to represent in his mind the red as it truly is? Never. Or someone who has never tried the strawberry, can he evoke it's exact flavor just listening to descriptions of it? Never.

So, the role of art is to recall overwhelming emotions that go beyond words. But art is not the emotion itself, nor the direct expression of it, but a symbol or representation of it. Direct expression of feelings through language is not possible, indeed, and the closest form is to say: "Oh...!" or "How beautiful!". This is the expressive function of language. But "Oh" is not a symbol of anything, but a mere onomatopoeia of a vocal emanation that proceeds from a particular psychic state of the person. In other words, it's not the emotion *represented* but only the physiological response to a particular emotion, just as the crying of a baby, to recall again an example given by the philosopher Susanne Langer. She also explains, very convincingly, that one goes not to a concert hall to listen babies crying, no matter how expressive and emotional it could be. This is because feeling in itself is not equal to beauty. On the contrary, it's usually rude and disturbing. I suppose no one would consider a beautiful thing to see in real life a mother crying over his son's coffin. Bot in art ti Gould be a sublime scene. Why so? Because what we admire in a great work of art is the mastery of representing accurately through an image, a musical passage, a metaphor, etc., the indefinable emotions we've had in the deepest and darkest region of our spirits. But if the artist would only say "Oh my God...!" or "Great!" this would be nothing out of the ordinary, or even out of the limited linguistic expressions all of us have. What would we need art for then if we can do ourselves the same thing? But what we can't do is to give tangible form to a deep feeling of our souls.

Now, almost every form of expression is a system of symbols. In the case of articulate language, the symbols are arbitrary and don't have any material relation with the objects symbolized. The word "book" was established arbitrarily to call to the mind the object with pastes and pages that corresponds to that sound. But in Spanish a very different sound ("libro") recalls exactly the same object. On the contrary, the artistic language, different from articulate language, is not a system of symbols or conventions, but in every work a new symbol is created, and must have a direct relation with the object signified in order to be accessible. There are, it is true, some conventions to produce sadness or joy, or some other common feeling in art. The painter knows colors and forms that could produce a certain emotion, and the musician knows that major and minor modes will recreate a determinate feeling in the spectator, but the principle remains, that every new work of true art represents a particular, ineffable emotion, becoming thus a new symbol corresponding only to that new emotion.

It's not clear why some emotions have more power over our souls than others, but this is undoubtedly so. Charles Baudelaire gives his opinion on this matter:

> *Je ne prétends pas que la joie ne puisse pas s'associer avec la beauté ; mais je dis que la joie est un des ornements les plus vulgaires, tandis que la mélancolie en est, pour ainsi dire, l'illustre compagne,*

á ce point, que je ne conçois guère un
type de beauté ou il n'y est de malheur.[14]

Apparently, and strangely, melancholy
has always been considered a higher feeling by
most great artists. The other two great feelings
that have been always present in history of art,
competing in highness with melancholy, are
majesty/heroism, and love. Joy and laughter
have always been somehow inferior, as the
French poet expressed. Comedy has always
been a kind of less profound beauty than trag-
edy or epic. These last two genres include religious and mystical feelings, repose, peace, etc.

The garden is a place full of emotions: the
nostalgia of a familiar smell or flower, the hap-
piness of a little meandering stream with alpine
flowers, the melancholy of a quiet, shadowy
pond or a wide and long, formal path covered

---

[14] I don't pretend that joy cannot be associated
with beauty, but I only say that joy is one of the most
vulgar onaments, while melancholy is, so to say, it's ilus-
trious companion, even to a point, that I can hardly con-
ceive a kind of beauty without disgrace.

with autumn leaves, the sublimity and majesty of an old tree or a powerful fountain, are just a few examples of how emotion can be present in every single corner of a garden.

3.- Ideology

The most "spiritual", less material product of the spirit is the idea. In emotions there is
still a reminiscence of bodily interaction. And
sometimes much more than only a reminiscence. What distinguishes man from animals is
not the capacity to express emotions, but to for-
mulate ideas. These ideas form, in every mind,
an ideology. The origin of every one´s ideology
has been under discussion for long time. Some
think it lies in the socio-economical level, others believe it is purely determined by the historical situation; others, yet, believe it comes
from nature. In reality all this factors, plus others, contribute to form an ideology in every artist or human being. Ideology is considered a
subjective appreciation of reality or, in other
words, an opinion. But this opinion can be
more or less accurate or truthful, according to
the method by which it was acquired. The fact
is that every artist has lots of opinions, and
even the pretended "pure" work has an ideology, being at least the ideology of the "pure

art", to call it somehow. So even the "lack" of ideology is an ideology in itself, and to disdain the intellectual part of art is an intellectual, but feeble, position in itself. So, the best thing an artist can do, knowing beforehand that his opinions will necessarily flow out through his works, is to improve his intellect, and to be sure of why he thinks what he thinks about life.

Now, the problem with ideology in art is not easy. For centuries a sharp debate has been kept among aestheticians on whether the ideological part enriches or impoverishes beauty. Philosophers have considered art, in relation with knowledge and science, from different points of view. Some have seen art as an inferior, even confuse or primitive, kind of knowledge, while others have thought, on the contrary, that art is a higher and more perfect form of science, letting us to intuit at least a little fragment of the Absolute. Some art of our time has failed in many senses because it has become an essentially intellectualist art, neither exceeding philosophical or scientific knowledge, nor reaching the great beauty that can lead us to experiment any absolute. This is just the opposite of the Romantic theory, in which the aesthetical activities are considered as something completely different from knowledge or intellectual issues, but more like dreaming and considering the intellect as a hindrance to the free movements of the soul.

But art is neither a "confuse or primitive knowledge", nor a philosophical treatise. It is similar to ideology in that they have common foundations, both trying to apprehend the total contents of life in all it's richness. But the difference is that art is aimed more to grasp the *unconscious* part of experience, while science is aimed to reduce knowledge to logical and articulate formulations. Art uses game, fantasy and fiction not only to escape from reality, but rather to go deeper onto it.

Printed in Great Britain
by Amazon

24198551R00055